Juan Radrigán

CHILDREN OF FATE
(HECHOS CONSUMADOS)

Translated by Robert Shaw

OBERON BOOKS
LONDON

WWW.OBERONBOOKS.COM

First published in 2013 by Oberon Books Ltd
521 Caledonian Road, London N7 9RH
Tel: +44 (0) 20 7607 3637 / Fax: +44 (0) 20 7607 3629
e-mail: info@oberonbooks.com
www.oberonbooks.com

A catalogue record for this book is available from the British
Library.

PB ISBN: 978-1-78319-073-7
E ISBN: 978-1-78319-572-5

Characters

MARTA

EMILIO

AURELIO

MIGUEL

'Anyone who wants to live has got to change the world.'

Wasteland on the edge of the city. Rocks, scrub, refuse etc. Stage left we make out the shape of a person (MARTA) asleep, covered with an old overcoat. Beside her, seated on a rock, a man is heating water on a small fire. Nearby, from a washing line improvised between two sticks, hang a blouse, a skirt, a jumper and a pair of stockings: two sacks can also be seen, one for flour, one for potatoes, both of them are half-full. It's a cold, grey evening.

The woman tosses and turns uneasily, she mumbles in her sleep: the man gets up and bends over her, intensely concerned. He listens for a moment. Suddenly he stiffens, as if he had heard or noticed something around him. He jumps up startled and goes to investigate. He takes a few steps, trying to get a better view.

The woman wakes with a start. She stares at him uncomprehending. She searches for something with her eyes.

MARTA: Wh…where's Mario?

EMILIO: *(Not looking at her.)* Oh hello there, lucky you woke up, I was starting to get worried about you.

MARTA: What happened?

EMILIO: I thought I heard someone moving around, *(He has another look.)* but I can't see anyone.

MARTA: No, I mean what happened. Where's Mario?

EMILIO: What Mario? There was only you. *(Sits back down.)*

MARTA: *(After a pause.)* Yeah. *(She smiles in apology.)* I was dreaming. *(Pause.)* What about you?

EMILIO: No, I'm not dreaming.

MARTA: I mean who are you, where did you spring from?

EMILIO: *(Waves his hand vaguely.)* Over there

MARTA: *(Looking round.)* Over where?

EMILIO: *(Flatly.)* I dunno.

MARTA: What do you mean you don't know?

EMILIO: I dunno. There's no signposts round here.

MARTA: What's the time?

EMILIO: Evening. Dunno what day it is.

MARTA: Jesus, how come you don't even know that?

EMILIO: Dunno, is all.

MARTA: You angry?

EMILIO: No. *(He stirs the fire.)* I just don't like talking.

MARTA: Why not? What else is there to do? *(She points excitedly out in front of them.)* Hey, look, look at them lot? Who are they? Where are they going? *(EMILIO looks without replying.)* You with them?

EMILIO: *(Smiling.)* How can I be with them if I'm sat here?

MARTA: No, mate: I mean are you with them, but did you sit down here for a cup of tea.

EMILIO: No, I haven't got a clue who they or where they're going.

MARTA: I don't like it. I'm frightened… Something must've happened.

EMILIO: You dunno what's been happening?

MARTA: What've I just said?

EMILIO: I can't hear what they're saying, *(Looking.)* but they don't look frightened to me.

MARTA: Don't look too happy, neither.

EMILIO: Don't expect too much, girl. If we all went around looking happy all the time, we'd get locked up. *(Gets out his cigarettes.)* Smoke?

MARTA: No, only sometimes. *(Putting on the overcoat.)* Fuck me, it's cold.

EMILIO: *(Lights the cigarette from the fire.)* It's freezing…

MARTA: You live round here?

EMILIO: No.

MARTA: Do they have to put something on your face to stop it hurting?

EMILIO: My face?

MARTA: Well yeah, I mean your jaw must be aching the whole time, you talk so much.

EMILIO: *(Laughs.)* What do you want me to say?

MARTA: I want to know what I'm doing here.

EMILIO: You're sitting here asking stupid questions.

MARTA: But how come I'm here? I don't remember anything.

EMILIO: You were drowning, I pulled you out of the canal, you've been asleep ever since. *(Pause.)* Did you jump or did you fall? *(MARTA doesn't answer. She shrugs her shoulders.)* Ah, so you jumped. *(He pours water from the can into a mug and hands it to her.)* Go on, it's good and hot.

MARTA: *(Blows on it. Takes a few sips in silence. To herself.)* Yeah, I guess I've lost track because of all the trouble last night… It's evening, you say?

EMILIO: *(Waving his hand.)* Make up your own mind.

MARTA: So how long have I been asleep?

EMILIO: I found you 'bout one in the morning and you've only just woken up so work it out for yourself.

MARTA: And you've been looking after me all that time?

EMILIO: *(Getting up.)* What else was I going to do? Lucky it didn't rain, it was well rough last night.

MARTA: *(Looking round.)* But it's nice now, isn't it?

EMILIO: Nice? Can't you see what a shit day it is? It's raining right now. Water must've got right onto your brain.

MARTA: I'm not listening. You got an attitude problem, you have. *(Looking round.)* It's nice.

EMILIO: *(Abruptly.)* What did you see? What could you see?

MARTA: *(Surprised, suspicious.)* When?

EMILIO: Before I pulled you out.

MARTA: *(Feeling trapped.)* Nothing.

EMILIO: What do you mean nothing? You were practically
gone. Try and remember. Did you feel afraid?

MARTA: No.

EMILIO: Peaceful?

MARTA: No.

EMILIO: Happy? Was it like you were gonna have a rest?

MARTA: No, no I didn't feel anything.

EMILIO: *(Getting worked up.)* You must've felt something. You
must've seen something.

MARTA: Go and ask them if you're so interested.

EMILIO: *(Taken aback.)* Who?

MARTA: *(In surprise.)* Why are you asking me?

EMILIO: Because you got a peep at somewhere we're all gonna
have to go. Who do you want me ask?

MARTA: *(Evasive.)* No, nothing.

EMILIO: It's like we're talking about different things.

MARTA: *(With spirit.)* No, it's the same thing; we're talking
about the same thing. It's just I didn't see anything. It's the
truth, I didn't see or feel anything. You think I was taking
notes under water?

EMILIO: They say you can see it. First your whole life passes
in front of your eyes and then you see something.

MARTA: *(Regaining control.)* I've told you already. If you're so
interested, why don't you jump in yourself.

EMILIO: *(Going to rekindle the fire.)* Maybe I will… But it's
weird though, when there's nothing to live for, there's
nothing to die for, neither. *(Pause.)* And anyway, if we're

so much trouble to them, why don't they finish what they started?

MARTA: *(Sharply. Walking up and down trying to work out where she is.)* I don't like that sort of talk. I like life.

EMILIO: So what you want to kill yourself for, then? 'Cause you were so blinking happy you'd just got yourself a new car?

MARTA: *(Rounding on him violently.)* I don't... *(Changing her mind.)* You shouldn't be asking me this. I don't even know your name.

EMILIO: It's Emilio. What's yours?

MARTA: What do you do?

EMILIO: You think even if there was any work, they'd give it to someone looking like me?

MARTA: Where do you live?

EMILIO: Wherever I can.

MARTA: And what were you before?

EMILIO: I think I was a person. Why are you asking me all this? Don't you trust me?

MARTA: It's just that... *(She goes up to him and gazes at him.)* No, you're not a bad person, you've got eyes like an abandoned dog.

EMILIO: What do you mean?

MARTA: I mean you've got double trouble – you're a dog and you're abandoned.

EMILIO: Oh, thanks a lot.

MARTA: No, I'm not being funny, it's just how you look. *(Starts walking up and down again.)* So, tell me again, where are we?

EMILIO: In your favourite place – life. Only not in the middle. More on the edge, really.

MARTA: I'm being serious. Can't you see I haven't a clue where I am?

EMILIO: I can't tell you any more. I don't pay attention to where I'm going any more. What's the point?

MARTA: Blimey, you're a barrel of laughs, aren't you. Bet you have them all in stitches down the soup kitchen.

EMILIO: Do you really like life?

MARTA: Yeah. Only thing is, it can't even see me.

EMILIO: Other way round with me. It likes me and I don't like it. *(Pause.)* We'd all be a lot fucking happier if you didn't need two people to fall in love.

MARTA: *(Short pause.)* I don't want to talk about love, it'll make me sad. *(Walking up and down.)* It's not the right moment for feeling sad. It feels like Sunday. No, it doesn't feel like Sunday at all, it feels like dawn is breaking…

EMILIO: Look at the state of us; old, pig-headed and barking.

MARTA: Speak for yourself. You need to get to know me better, before you can be rude to me.

EMILIO: I don't mean you, I'm talking about life. It makes you so happy, you can't even find somewhere to drop dead.

MARTA: Have you finished, at all?

EMILIO: I'm not being rude; it's the truth.

MARTA: OK, if me being happy bothers you so much, I could poke one of my eyes out with a stick, or I could shove my head under a lorry. *(She laughs. Distant sound of cans.)*

EMILIO: What's that?

MARTA: *(Pointing towards the back.)* It's coming from over there…

(AURELIO emerges out of the night. He is a strange being. The rags he is wearing are nondescript; in fact they aren't rags, there's a subtle difference between something worn out by time and something

destroyed by rubbing, by daily use; his clothes are worn out by time. A few empty cans hang from his body.)

MARTA: *(Quietly.)* He's a headcase.

EMILIO: No, he's just a bloke. *(AURELIO stares at them from a distance.)*

MARTA: Jesus, look at his clothes.

EMILIO: He probably thinks the same about us… Thinking differently… That's what we all call madness. *(To AURELIO.)* How are you, mate?

AURELIO: Hungry.

MARTA: *(With sympathy. To EMILIO.)* Have you got any bread?

AURELIO: No, no bread. *(He approaches them, pointing at the fire.)* Can I?

MARTA: Sure, come closer. *(To EMILIO.)* Give him some room.

AURELIO: *(Settling down.)* No, I'm fine right here.

EMILIO: You'd be more comfortable if you took your armour off.

AURELIO: *(Steps backwards in fear. Hugs himself violently, protecting the cans.)* No, I can't, they keep me safe!

EMILIO: What from?

MARTA: It doesn't matter. *(To AURELIO.)* If you don't want to take them off then don't. He just meant it looked like they were bothering you. Have you come far?

AURELIO: *(Approaches the fire once more.)* Yes, from a long way away, from nowhere.

MARTA: How's that?

AURELIO: From the arsehole of the world.

MARTA: And you're just passing through, are you?

EMILIO: No, she means how can you come from nowhere?

AURELIO: *(Abruptly.)* What are you doing here?

MARTA: Here? *(She shrugs her shoulders.)* Nothing, really.

AURELIO: How did you get to this place?

EMILIO: She swam here, I came from the same place you did, more or less. Why?

AURELIO: *(Almost to himself.)* You must have found something. Nobody stays anywhere without a reason. What have you found?

MARTA: No, we haven't found anything, have we, Emilio?

AURELIO: *(Gets up and sniffs the air.)* If you stopped here, it means you must have found something... Do you really not know what you've found?

EMILIO: No we really don't. What is there to find here? This is just wasteland.

AURELIO: There must be something for you here. *(He points to the cans.)* They're ringing. It's a sign.

MARTA: Do they tell you your future?

AURELIO: There's no such thing, lady. There are people, rivers, stars, wind, flowers and knives. Everything has a name and an inevitable fate.

MARTA: And what's my fate?

AURELIO: Living, lady.

MARTA: Yeah, but how?

AURELIO: *(Harshly.)* I want to know what you've found here. Tell me, it's important, tell me.

EMILIO: Don't get stroppy, mate, we just...

AURELIO: *(Rattles the cans, listens. Stares at them pityingly.)* Everything you have fits into a fist or into a shout... Empty flagons and a wailing inside you, always inside you, always there inside you... The old dream of a quiet place, that inward torrent unable to flood out into the world, always inside you, always there inside you...

MARTA: *(Quietly, to EMILIO.)* What's he on about?

EMILIO: We're always inside, we're always there inside us.

AURELIO: *(Rattles the cans. Listens. Gloomy.)* Water… Bones crushed against the sky… The black water of death… *(Restlessly.)* Night's closing in. I'm going. *(Makes a hand gesture.)*

MARTA: What did you see? What did you see in the cans?

AURELIO: Nothing. They told me nothing. *(Questioning spirits from another world.)* Why here? Why here?

MARTA: What about here? What did you see?

AURELIO: Is showing them the way the same as following their footsteps?

EMILIO: Listen you freak, if you know something, stop talking riddles and say it out loud.

MARTA: If you've seen something, tell us.

AURELIO: *(Pointing to him.)* This man is gaining the dimensions of death! *(He rattles the tins in an increasing rhythm, as if refusing to believe. He listens. Stunned.)* The wind of injustice howls once more… For how long? Why? *(Pause.)* It howls and it howls… What's it seeking now? For how long? *(Pause.)* Where is the bread and the corn?

What happened to the cosmic joy of giving birth? Did we sweat our lives away for nothing? So much death and nothing, so much death and nothing! *(Distressed.)* I will never return to the city… I'll never be able to go back… *(One of the tins on his body rattles as if by accident. He remains motionless, listening, his expression changes, he becomes cheerful. He rattles them.)* It comes all in white and smiling: death is coming in smiling. Of course, everything that falls is reborn purified… Oh God, at last you decided to keep mankind on high… Will it be here? Will it only be here? I must go and see, I must go and see! *(He exits jumping.)*

MARTA: *(Following him for a short way.)* Hey, come back!

EMILIO: Leave him.

MARTA: Was he crazy?

EMILIO: What do you reckon?

MARTA: I think he was!

EMILIO: So why you asking me?

MARTA: Doesn't it bother you though?

EMILIO: If he's right, I got nowhere to hide and if he ain't, I've got nothing to worry about?

MARTA: Yeah, and why did he say he was hungry if he didn't want anything to eat?

EMILIO: Yeah, well he's stuffed right there isn't he because the only bread that cures all hunger is justice and you can whistle for that round here.

MARTA: Blimey, and he went that way: the poor mad bastard'll probably fall into the canal to cap it all off.

EMILIO: No, the canal's that way, it goes like this.

MARTA: *(Astonished.)* That way? How come we're so far away?

EMILIO: It's not as cold here.

MARTA: And how did you manage to carry me so far?

EMILIO: On my shoulders.

MARTA: Yeah…and was I…was I dressed?

EMILIO: Yeah course you were, or did you think I packed you a suitcase? I took them off you. I pulled you out of the canal, I wasn't going to let you die of pneumonia. *(He points to the clothes.)* Put them on.

MARTA: They're still wet.

EMILIO: They're dry, I dried them for you by the fire.

MARTA: What did you do that for?

EMILIO: Because they were wet.

MARTA: No, I mean…no one's ever done anything for me. People always just avoid me… And you looked after me and dried my clothes… Thanks.

EMILIO: *(After a short pause.)* No problem. Next time you jump in the water, come and see me afterwards and I'll dry them for you again. Do you live far away?

MARTA: I don't have a home… Ever since Mario dumped me I've been on my own.

EMILIO: Is that why you were trying to wash your clothes with you still inside them?

MARTA: No, that was something different.

EMILIO: What?

MARTA: Just different. *(Pause.)* Mario left a long time ago, a long time ago; it'll be three months soon…

EMILIO: Where did he go?

MARTA: Maybe he's dead. *(Goes over to the clothes and feels them.)* They really are dry. I'm going to put them on. *(Stares at him.)* Turn round like a good boy.

EMILIO: *(Pointing.)* They'll see you. And there are young children too.

MARTA: *(Looking.)* OK, so stand in front of me. *(EMILIO gets up and stands in front of her.)* And now look the other way, cheeky.

EMILIO: You see, I can be cheeky when I want. *(He turns round.)* This Mario, was he your…?

MARTA: He was my companion.

EMILIO: Did he die or was he killed?

MARTA: *(Getting dressed.)* I don't know… Well, anyway he's dead as far as I'm concerned. He left me high and dry. Did he die or was he killed? I've never thought about that. One day he grabbed his tools, looked at me and said 'You know something? You're a complete waste of space', and then he just left. We'd been together more than six years.

EMILIO: And you didn't say anything?

MARTA: What was I supposed I say? I don't beg, for bed or food. Anyway, words are no use at times like that, because if you have to make yourself say it, it's not love.

EMILIO: You've got your pride, then.

MARTA: No, it's not pride, love's got to be real not pretend. I'm a real person. *(She's finished getting dressed.)* OK, you can turn round if you want, you can look now. *(EMILIO turns round and stares at her. MARTA is embarrassed.)* I mean just a quick look.

EMILIO: You look beautiful. The only thing is, you look like you ironed your clothes with a brick. *(He freezes, he seems to be listening.)*

MARTA: What's the matter?

EMILIO: Do you get the feeling we're been watched? It feels like someone's moving around out there? *(Looks around.)*

MARTA: *(Scared, following him.)* It's the headcase!

EMILIO: No.

MARTA: *(Pointing.)* That lot!

EMILIO: *(Searching, sniffing the air.)* That's different… I felt it a little while ago, too.

MARTA: I can't see anyone. There are no trees or big rocks, there's nowhere for anyone to hide.

EMILIO: *(Darkly.)* There's someone there… Someone's wandering around out there.

MARTA: Are you in any trouble?

EMILIO: I don't think so. You never know though, do you? What about you?

MARTA: I don't know. I talk. I laugh. Is that bad?

EMILIO: Depends.

MARTA: If only we knew what was allowed and what wasn't?

EMILIO: They couldn't tell us that. *(Pause.)*

MARTA: Maybe we should get out of here.

EMILIO: Where to?

MARTA: Yes, always the same problem. Why do they harass us?

EMILIO: Because they're making a better world.

MARTA: Better for who?

EMILIO: For us, of course.

MARTA: And how are they doing that?

EMILIO: *(Sitting down.)* You have to find that out for yourself.

MARTA: And how will it be better?

EMILIO: That's what we'd all like to know. *(Pause.)* Do you have any children?

MARTA: No… Well, I was pregnant once, but I lost it. *(She shrugs her shoulders.)* Anyway, Mario didn't want any. *(She stands in thought.)* It must be great to have a child, don't you think? I've noticed women always seem to glow when they're holding a child. *(She mimes that.)*

EMILIO: It's a beautiful thing… Especially when they ask for something to eat and you've got nothing to give them. 'The children of the poor are healthy and robust, because they grow up next to the earth and walk about naked.' Have you ever heard that?

MARTA: Yeah, those ignorant toffs are always talking rubbish like that.

EMILIO: Good thing your husband had some sense.

MARTA: *(Haughtily.)* Mario wasn't my husband, we were just together. *(Pause.)* But even if he was, I'd already realised we couldn't have one because we'd nowhere to bring it up. Fuck it, God should have…

EMILIO: Don't blame Him. He doesn't share things out, he just makes them: other people share them out.

MARTA: Yeah, I know how things get shared out… One time, they came to our house and started chucking everything outside. My mother grabbed us and hid in a corner: 'Just take it all, you bastards' she said to them, 'but don't you ask me anything'. She taught me never to beg, she taught me to smack myself in the face with a rock before I should beg.

EMILIO: Why did they take your things? When was that?

MARTA: A long time ago, I was about ten. *(Pause.)* But I don't like talking about it, it upsets me. Do you have children?

EMILIO: I did have.

MARTA: Are they dead?

EMILIO: Yes, they're completely dead.

MARTA: What do you mean?

EMILIO: They've forgotten all about me.

MARTA: And what about you?

EMILIO: What about me?

MARTA: Have you forgotten about them, too?

EMILIO: What are you going to do?

MARTA: *(After a short pause.)* I don't know. Move on.

EMILIO: And do you have anywhere to live?

MARTA: No.

EMILIO: Then you'll get there dead quick.

MARTA: *(Pointing excitedly.)* Look, there's a fire! *(They stand up and look.)*

EMILIO: What's burning?

MARTA: I know that kind of smoke… It's when they burn grass or corn.

EMILIO: They either burn it or they fence it off. *(He goes and sits down.)*

MARTA: Do you know any toff with a house and garden?

EMILIO: A garden? No, why?

MARTA: You could give me the address. Looking after gardens is what I do. That's what me and Mario used to do for a living…

EMILIO: Gardens? Are there any left?

MARTA: Not many. *(Pause.)* It makes me really mad: people lock themselves inside their houses and let their gardens die.

EMILIO: That must be the reason.

MARTA: But it was worse… Carnations, daisies, dahlias, they're all in season right now. Then come the gladioli and the double chrysanths. The colours all looked so wonderful… But people've just let their gardens dry up and I wanna know what are people going to do when spring comes round and there are no more flowers?

EMILIO: If there's no land to walk on or bread to eat, I don't think people care about that much right now.

MARTA: You're like all the rest, you blame all your troubles on the big things, but it's the little things, the things that look as if they don't matter, that's what pushes you over the edge. *(EMILIO doesn't answer. MARTA takes a few steps and stops in front of him)* Well, thanks for everything.

EMILIO: No problem. *(Silence.)*

MARTA: *(Pointing.)* Is the road that way?

EMILIO: No, you need to go the other way. *(Points.)*

MARTA: Do they come from the city?

EMILIO: Probably.

31

MARTA: Have they escaped?

EMILIO: I don't think so. They look very quiet. What I mean is you have to go towards where they came from; soon you'll start to notice a rotting smell; follow that smell and you'll find the city.

MARTA: And what are you going to do?

EMILIO: *(He gets out his cigarettes.)* Right now, I'm going to have a smoke. After that, I don't know.

MARTA: *(After a pause. Pointing to the mug.)* You know? I think I'll have that cup of tea before I go… I've no money to get one later.

EMILIO: If you're going to have one, put the water on the fire. It's gone cold.

MARTA: *(Sitting down.)* OK, I will. Do you want one?

EMILIO: No.

MARTA: *(Searching for something to say.)* Cold, isn't it?

EMILIO: Yeah

MARTA: Will it rain?

EMILIO: I dunno.

MARTA: Where do you go when it rains?

EMILIO: Somewhere I don't get wet.

MARTA: *(She laughs.)* No, really. *(Pause.)* We're a long way from anywhere, aren't we? *(EMILIO stands up without answering.)* Where are you going?

EMILIO: To get something for the fire. It's going out.

MARTA: *(Gesture of getting up.)* I'll go.

EMILIO: No, you stay and look after the sacks.

He starts to search. He picks up the odd branch, the odd piece of paper, he then disappears. MARTA stands, looks at her clothes, tries to smooth them, to arrange her hair etc. Then she picks up the overcoat, folds it carefully and moves the sacks. She takes a stick from the washing line and uses it like a broom to sweep the place. People going by attract her attention. She stands and stares at them. She takes a few steps towards them.

MARTA: *(Shouting.)* Hey… Where've you come from? Where are you going? Answer me, answer me. Who are you? Who are you?

She waits, she shrugs her shoulders, she carries on sweeping. EMILIO enters with branches, pieces of plank, anything combustible. He stands and looks at her, perplexed.

EMILIO: What are you doing?

MARTA: Cleaning.

EMILIO: Why?

MARTA: To make it clean. *(She smiles.)* We women are always cleaning.

EMILIO: But… For God's sake, why do you want start cleaning round here. This is hardly a house.

MARTA: If you don't have a house, wherever you happen to be, that's your house.

EMILIO: *(Drops the rubbish.)* Don't be daft.

MARTA: Jesus, what's wrong? *(She throws away the stick.)* I won't touch a thing then!

EMILIO: Have you always been in such a good mood?

MARTA: I'm just me. No one humiliates me.

EMILIO: *(Pleased.)* Brilliant! I love you like that. If I was wearing a hat, I'd take it off to you, I swear I would.

MARTA: Are you taking the piss?

EMILIO: No, I mean it. They can kick you, they can take everything you can have, but that's OK, you've still got your pride. But if they take your dignity, then you've lost it all, because then you're nothing, not even a piece of shit, you get me?

MARTA: More or less.

EMILIO: No, listen. Once upon a time, a door opened somewhere and all the evil in the world came rushing in. Jesus Christ himself couldn't save you from hunger, or loneliness or the devil. But dignity can keep you from turning into an animal. Don't matter what it costs, that's all there is.

MARTA: So with dignity or without it, I'm still the walking dead. Jesus, you know how to give a girl hope. With all your faith in life, you should get a job sitting with patients in a hospital, you'd make a fortune.

EMILIO: That's just how I am, I feel so good inside, I wish I could offer you something better, but this is all there is.

MARTA: Offer me? Are you trying to tell me something?

EMILIO: No, I'm just talking.

MARTA: You ever had your own house?

EMILIO: *(Steps forward, looks around.)* Yeah, a long time ago. *(He points.)* I asked one of them where they were going, but he pretended not to understand. I mean he stared at me like I was thick or something... When you get close to them, they look tired, they look...

MARTA: Do you miss them?

EMILIO: Who?

MARTA: I don't know. Your wife?

EMILIO: Course I do. But what can I do about it, what's lost is lost. You have to learn how to have nothing.

MARTA: But we're not animals. Maybe it hurts sometimes, but love...

EMILIO: Love? If a woman can't put bread on the table, a man can't get into her bed; that's love. We thought we had something but no... What kept us together was bread, bed and needing company, but there was no love. *(MARTA tries to protest.)* No don't wave your hands at me, you go there *(Pointing.)* go to that damn city and see who's staying together. Just people who've still got a job or maybe just loads of money.

MARTA: That's so cynical. And there's me not trusting you because I thought you wanted something! *(She laughs.)* Don't be silly. I know it's hard but...

EMILIO: Are you trying to give me advice? I'm still young and good-looking enough to find someone, is that it?

MARTA: Course I'm not, but why cry about what you can't change? Anyway, if it wasn't for you, who would someone like me have to talk to? The only person who can comfort someone down on their luck is someone else down on their luck, so don't be dumb.

And just so you know, no one can say they'll never fall in love again, because your heart doesn't give a shit about what you think, it just goes and falls in love. So don't go getting big ideas.

EMILIO: How come you know so much about love?

MARTA: Because I love life. There are times when my heart aches for what I see around me, but I don't believe love is dead; good love is like a good plant, it doesn't grow on its own, you have to look after it if you want it to flourish. No, I'll teach you... *(Startled.)* Where did he come from? Is he looking for the headcase?

EMILIO: *(Looking.)* Who?

MARTA: *(Quietly.)* Him. Shhh... *(From the pit a man appears – MIGUEL – with a club. In a friendly voice.)* Good evening.

MIGUEL: Evening.

MARTA: Are you looking for someone?

MIGUEL: *(Watches without answering. Enters. Pokes/pushes the stick on the ground with his club.)* There's only you is there?

EMILIO: Is that yours?

MARTA: Do you want to sit by the fire?

MIGUEL: *(Not looking at them.)* Are you from round here?

EMILIO: What's that got to do with you?

MARTA: No, we're not from round here, we're just passing through. Where did you spring from?

MIGUEL: *(Vaguely.)* Over there *(Pause.)* Have you finished your tea?

MARTA: I've not had any yet. *(Pause.)* How did you know we were having tea?

MIGUEL: It's my job to know everything. *(Pause.)* Just drink your tea. *(Leaving.)* It's not time yet.

MARTA: Time for what? *(MIGUEL doesn't answer. He vanishes. To EMILIO.)* Time for what, did he say?

EMILIO: Maybe he did.

MARTA: Don't be such a pain. And you were rude to him. You should be more careful. Couldn't you see he could be dangerous?

EMILIO: I don't like people who carry weapons or people who creep up on you. Always ends in violence.

MARTA: But you shouldn't go around confronting people.

EMILIO: I don't confront people. I can't make anyone love me or give me a job or somewhere to live. But I can certainly make sure no one walks all over me. If they can't make me do something I don't want to do, they can't make me do anything. In the end, that's all there is. You can worship your stupid fucking love and your stupid fucking hope all you want, just let me be who I am.

MARTA: *(Angry.)* I don't worship anything just shut your mouth.

EMILIO: You tried to kill yourself.

MARTA: No, I didn't!

EMILIO: So what were you doing in the canal? Learning to swim?

MARTA: *(Looking round on all sides.)* It wasn't me. I was thrown in.

EMILIO: Thrown in? Who by? Mario?

MARTA: Keep your voice down!

EMILIO: Don't be scared. Don't be scared any more. Who threw you in?

MARTA: I don't know. I don't know who they were, I was so scared I didn't get a good look at them. *(Almost gaily.)* Anyway, I was crying so much.

EMILIO: Crying? Then you lied to me. You told me you never begged.

MARTA: I didn't beg them, I was just crying. It was a trick I thought of to try and get them to leave me alone.

EMILIO: And what were you doing for them to pick you up like that?

MARTA: Just being alive in the wrong place, that's what I was doing. I had the bad luck to be walking down a street where three guys were dragging a bundle out of an alleyway and I froze. I got the willies. *(Pause.)* Do you know what the willies are?

EMILIO: No.

MARTA: Like Chavo del Ocho

EMILIO: Who's that?

MARTA: Chavo del Siete's brother. *(She laughs.)*

EMILIO: You're winding me up.

MARTA: No, it's a Mexican sitcom. I used to watch it when I was going round doing the gardens with Mario. It was all about this crazy guy who when he got scared would go all stiff and twisted, like this *(She imitates Chavo del Ocho – she freezes into an awkward stance with her knees bent, back slouched, left arm dropping down and right arm hanging out with only her hand dropping downward.)* That's just how I went when I saw these blokes. Then right away one of them came up to me and said:

'You, what are you doing here? Are you spying on us?'

'No, sir', I said, 'I was only passing by.'

'Where do you live?'

'I don't have a home,' I said, 'Since Mario left me, I've been on my own.'

'OK,' he said, 'Get lost. You can go.'

I was just moving on, really happy, when one of the others who seemed to be in charge said:

'No. No, we can't take the risk.'

'But the bitch doesn't know anything,' he said.

'No, listen to me, we can't take the risk she might go shooting her mouth off. Get her in.'

And then they grabbed me and shoved me in the car too. That's when I got the idea about crying. 'What's your name? What are your politics? How long have you been getting yourself into trouble?' they said to me. So I started crying and crying.

EMILIO: What was the bundle they threw in the car?

MARTA: It was moving, but I couldn't see it too well. I spent the whole time crying. They even gave me a good kicking to try and get me to stop, but I didn't let up. We'd been going for a good while when one of them said to the others:

'Fucking hell, this bitch is driving me crazy with her wailing, what are we going to do with her?' So the one in charge grabbed me by the hair and said:

'Right, you miserable cow, if you don't shut your trap, we'll kill you and throw you in that canal.'

But I wasn't going to stop for anything, if I stopped crying they could get me to say anything and then I'd be in real trouble. But I could see which way the wind was blowing, they weren't gonna get me to… *(She stops. They listen hard.)* You hear that?

EMILIO: Of course, sirens. *(They stand and watch.)*

MARTA: *(Fearfully.)* But they're not fire engines. They sound different.

EMILIO: Now what's happened?

MARTA: We should beat it.

EMILIO: No, wait. *(He points.)* The problem must be with them.

MARTA: But they'll pick us up too.

EMILIO: So what?

MARTA: I don't want to be killed! There they are, let's go. *(She takes him by the arm and pulls him.)*

EMILIO: *(Watching carefully.)* They're not running, they're not frightened. It doesn't seem like they've heard anything.

MARTA: They've gone! It wasn't them after all. So where are they going?

EMILIO: Someone's going to find out.

MARTA: Why didn't they run away? Why weren't they frightened?

EMILIO: I don't know. They must be pissed off with running away and being scared, they must have known it was nothing to do with them. *(Getting interested.)* He's having a go at them…

MARTA: *(Trying to see.)* What?

EMILIO: Over there in the distance. The guy with the club.

MARTA: So he is, he's arguing with them.

EMILIO: *(On an impulse.)* I'm going to take a look.

MARTA: *(Grabbing him.)* No, don't go… I'm scared, I don't want to be left alone.

EMILIO: Let me go, I've got nothing to do with you.

MARTA: And I've got nothing to do with you, what are you shouting at me for?

EMILIO: *(Surprised.)* Hey, they're not even taking any notice of the guy with the club.

MARTA: No, they're not… Who are they? Who are they?

EMILIO: I dunno; but whoever they are, they know what they're doing. And one day, little by little, they have to get somewhere. I guess that's what you have to do, I guess life has no purpose except the one you make for yourself.

MARTA: But they don't pay attention to anyone.

EMILIO: I like them, I'm beginning to like them.

MARTA: OK, you go with them if you like them so much.

EMILIO: Why did that guy just now think I knew what he was talking about? When they say, 'Don't play dumb', it means they're accusing you of something.

MARTA: What are you on about?

EMILIO: Are you angry with me?

MARTA: No, why would I be angry? You're free to do what you like. *(She sits down in EMILIO's place. She searches in the sack.)*

EMILIO: Do you want something to eat? I've got a few things in the other sack… *(Pensively.)* Where there's a will there's a way.

MARTA: *(She stops ferreting about in the sack.)* Now what are you on about?

EMILIO: *(Going right upstage.)* Just the usual. About how you have spend your life searching and searching…

MARTA: You're weird, you are.

EMILIO: Why weird?

MARTA: *(Stops to think.)* I dunno.

EMILIO: Don't listen to me then. *(Calming down.)* OK, you never finished telling me what happened to you.

MARTA: I don't want to remember. I only told you so you wouldn't think I threw myself in.

EMILIO: So they were just passing by, you caught them in the middle of something, they shoved you in the car and then they threw you in the canal, just like that, like a fag end or chucking out the rubbish.

MARTA: Yeah, just like that. But what happened, happened. I'm still alive. That's what matters. *(EMILIO starts to protest, she stands and goes towards him.)* No, don't argue. If you get too close to the fire you get burned. I don't want to learn how to be scared, I don't want to learn to cry... Being alive is beautiful, the earth is not to blame for anything. It's like a house without walls, it's got everything you need, everything you like, sun, plants, water, fruit, birds, everything. It's not to blame for... *(EMILIO silences her.)* What's the matter?

EMILIO: *(Pointing.)* He's coming this way again.

MARTA: *(Looking.)* Now what does he want? *(They stand, waiting. Enter MIGUEL. There is something imperceptibly threatening in his friendliness; something that cannot only be ascribed to the fact that he's carrying a club.)*

MIGUEL: Hello.

MARTA: Hello...

MIGUEL: *(Tucks the club away about his person. Rubs his hands.)* Cold evening, isn't it?

EMILIO: Well it's winter, isn't it? It'd be a surprise if it was hot.

MIGUEL: *(Smiling.)* Sure.

MARTA: Don't be rude.

MIGUEL: *(Still smiling.)* It's OK. *(Pause.)* Have you finished the tea?

EMILIO: I have, she hasn't.

MIGUEL: Aren't you together?

EMILIO: Oxen go round together.

MIGUEL: Are you angry, mate?

MARTA: No, he's just like that. He says he doesn't like talking and then you can't get him to shut up.

MIGUEL: *(Coming nearer. Deliberately.)* So then, looks like that's my job.

EMILIO: I don't think so.

MARTA: *(Quickly.)* Do you want some tea? Would you like some tea?

MIGUEL: No, thank you. I was only asking if you'd had any… It's just that I came around a little while ago, but as you hadn't finished your tea, I didn't want to disturb you.

EMILIO: How would you be disturbing us?

MIGUEL: Well, you see I'm the security guard. I've been sent to tell you that this is private property.

EMILIO: So?

MIGUEL: And that you can't stay here.

MARTA: Of course, we were just leaving… I mean he's going his way and I'm going mine.

EMILIO: Why can't we stay here?

MARTA: Because this isn't our property, he's just said. *(To MIGUEL.)* We weren't here on purpose. We didn't know it was private property.

EMILIO: The truth is, we didn't know the whole world was private property, that's why we were born. *(He sits down.)* If someone had taken the trouble to let us know…

MIGUEL: Why are you sitting down? I'm serious. *(EMILIO doesn't answer.)* I've let you stay here all day, you can't complain. *(To MARTA, who is trying to sit down.)* I'm being quite serious, madam.

MARTA: I'm not madam.

MIGUEL: Suit yourself. *(To EMILIO.)* Let's go.

EMILIO: *(Taking off a shoe.)* I can't go anywhere. I've twisted my foot.

MIGUEL: What do you mean you've twisted your foot, you were just standing there…

EMILIO: Funny that…

MIGUEL: Don't get clever with me, matey, I'm not in the mood. I came to talk to you nicely, I thought we could have a nice cup of tea and all, but don't push it.

MARTA: We've not said anything wrong, and we're going right now, as you're in such a hurry.

EMILIO: Why should we go? This is wasteland, we're not bothering anyone.

MIGUEL: I don't know, it's nothing to do with me: he sent me here to tell you he doesn't want to find you here when he gets here: I'm just the messenger.

MARTA: Who's 'he'?

MIGUEL: The boss.

MARTA: And when's he getting here?

MIGUEL: *(Almost offended.)* That's up to him.

EMILIO: Oh, so no rush then. *(To MARTA.)* Take your time; there's some stuff in the small sack.

MIGUEL: Oy, none of that, matey, don't make this hard: I don't want to have to hurt you.

EMILIO: So why do it then? *(To MARTA.)* Go on give him something and get something for me too.

MARTA: *(Weighing up the situation.)* We don't have anywhere to go. *(She starts poking around in the sack.)*

MIGUEL: *(Threateningly.)* Are you gonna do one?

MARTA: We've got nowhere to go.

MIGUEL: That's your problem, not mine. *(Brandishes the club.)* Get out of here now!

MARTA: *(Frightened.)* No, what's he doing?

MIGUEL: If you can't take a hint. I got a job to do!

MARTA: Careful, Emilio!

EMILIO: No, he the one who needs to be careful. *(To MIGUEL.)* Killing someone is no trouble mate, it only takes a minute or two. But then what? You got a home? You got a family? Think about that.

MIGUEL: You're on private property, I can do what I like.

EMILIO: Don't be daft, mate, if you kill us they'll crucify you. Didn't you know? If nothing happens between poor people, the law dies of hunger? The law is a very strange animal, mate, it doesn't dine on the finest meat, it likes skinny, rotting flesh, like yours and mine.

MIGUEL: Don't start, you may be a good bullshitter, but you're not fooling me. The boss has just sent me to say that he won't take crap from anyone, and I'm just doing what I've got to do.

MARTA: No one's arguing about that, you're doing what you have to do and we're doing what we have to do.

EMILIO: Yeah, you know, we don't want to make any trouble for you. Why would we do that, we're all in the same boat.

MIGUEL: I've got my house and my job, I don't go round trespassing on other people's property.

MARTA: Some people have all the luck. I used to do gardens, but who's got a garden for me to do now?

EMILIO: I used to be a weaver, but now they're importing everything, I can't even get a job knitting.

MIGUEL: You won't find anything sitting here all day. *(Setting aside his aggression a bit)* You were a weaver? What sort of thing?

EMILIO: Everything, blankets, cashmere, towels, whatever came my way.

MIGUEL: And where did you work?

EMILIO: Pff, where didn't I work! I had work in the 'Fresia' factory, in Comandari, in Polax, I even worked in the Jewish Women's Arcade over in Pedro Alarcón, that's the full story I'm giving you.

MIGUEL: Yeah, I know… I used to work in textiles… That is I still do.

EMILIO: Hey, that's great, so we're workmates.

MARTA: Well, almost. He's got a job.

EMILIO: Do you want some tea? Your hands look like they're going blue.

MARTA: *(Taking things out of the sack.)* A nice cup of tea and a bread sandwich you'll be right as rain.

EMILIO: Is there enough for three?

MIGUEL: No, I don't want any. I have to get back to work. Apart from being the security guard, I work with the wolf.

MARTA: You work with a wolf? Blimey, that's a dangerous job.

EMILIO: *(Smiling.)* No, it's a machine for working old bits of cloth.

MIGUEL: You do that too?

EMILIO: Sure, I know just about everything to do with working in textiles. *(To MARTA.)* It's a machine for making felt. It works with any old rags the boss can buy from the rubbish dumps; dirty and smelly rags, that give off this huge cloud of dust when you put them into the machine.

MIGUEL: That'd be where you worked. We don't work with rubbish, we use textile offcuts.

EMILIO: That's how it's supposed to be, but it never is. Does the machine ever get clogged up?

MIGUEL: Sometimes.

EMILIO: Well that's why. That's because of the buttons and the bits and pieces attached to the rags, they get into the works and they build up until the machine gets clogged. *(To MARTA.)* There are times you can't even see yourself for the dust. *(To MIGUEL.)* Do they give you trouble?

MIGUEL: *(Looking stealthily towards the place where he came from.)* No, why would they give us trouble?

EMILIO: And where is the machine? I can't hear it from here at all.

MIGUEL: *(Pointing.)* Over there; you have to turn left, over there, see those dogs poking about, more or less there, and then straight on.

EMILIO: That far…? And he owns all this as well?

MIGUEL: Not only. No one knows for sure what he's into.

EMILIO: And all from making felt?

MIGUEL: No, I'm telling you, not even I know everything he's into.

EMILIO: So how can we be bothering him if he's so powerful?

MIGUEL: I don't know, but he told me to say that he doesn't want to see you round here. *(Pause.)* So why make trouble for me, do you get my point?

MARTA: Do many people work in the felt factory? Maybe they've got work for us.

MIGUEL: Don't even dream about it. We're not taking anyone on right now. Work it out – out of fifteen master-weavers, we've just let five of them go. Even I'm having to work on the machines to cut costs. People don't understand that.

Sometimes I wonder what world they're living in; one
of my master-weavers has been off for a week now. I try
telling them to take their work seriously, but I might as
well be talking to myself.

MARTA: That's where he could fit in.

MIGUEL: No, that's the machine I'm working on myself.

EMILIO: I always got into trouble with the security guards… I
remember there was this one they called Palomo.

MIGUEL: The one who got chucked into the salad-spinner?

EMILIO: Yeah, did you know him?

MIGUEL: No, I just heard about him.

MARTA: What's a salad-spinner?

EMILIO: It's a machine for drying cloth after it's been dyed.

MARTA: And he got chucked inside?

EMILIO: Yeah, he was a right bastard. He was a carpenter, but
then he became a security guard and he was the biggest
bastard there's ever been… He got what was coming to
him.

MIGUEL: You have to see it from both sides. If they give you
responsibility, you have to take it. I mean, my boss has
given me instructions that people can't smoke during
working hours, they can't eat and they can't talk; and I
have to make sure they do it, that's what I'm paid for.

EMILIO: That must be tough.

MIGUEL: No, it all depends on everyone knowing their place,
as long as there's order then there's no problem. Anyway,
we don't force anyone to work for us; anyone who doesn't
like the work just leaves; why stay and cause trouble?

MARTA: I remember when I was doing the gardens with
Mario, we used to get three hundred pesos, food included.
But when things started to get bad, they stopped giving
us food; then they started paying us two hundred pesos,

and then one hundred… Take it or leave it. It wasn't half fucking tough!

MIGUEL: And what's that got to do with what anything?

MARTA: It's just that the bosses never showed their faces, they'd always send some minion to fuck us over. Why don't you sit down for a bit?

MIGUEL: No, I have to go. *(Pause.)* You will leave, won't you? No point in fighting.

MARTA: Yeah, sure we don't want to fight, we just want to live.

EMILIO: Unfortunately these days you have to fight to live. Sit down for a bit, she's just going to boil some water.

MIGUEL: *(Sits down.)* Just for a while. I've left my wife alone over there.

EMILIO: Would you have beaten us with that club?

MARTA: We've never done anything to you.

EMILIO: Would you have beaten us?

MIGUEL: I carry this club, because you never know who you're going to come across. *(Pause.)* It was the missus who made me bring it… She's sick, the dust from the machines has fucked her up…

MARTA: Shall I take her a little tea?

MIGUEL: No thanks. She won't open the door to you, she's stuck in bed. *(He points.)* And she's scared of that lot. *(The three of them talk and stare at the people.)*

EMILIO: They're still there.

MARTA: So many of them; old folks, children… Where are they going?

MIGUEL: I don't know, who knows?

EMILIO: But you were moving them along a little while ago.

MIGUEL: No, I wasn't moving them along. It's just I thought I saw that master-weaver I was talking about who's been off work … But I couldn't really see if it was him, and as he didn't answer…

MARTA: But you were carrying that club. Anyone would be scared.

MIGUEL: And anyone would be scared of them, too. They don't talk.

EMILIO: They don't ask anything.

MARTA: They're just walking.

EMILIO: I like them…

MIGUEL: I'm afraid of them, I'm afraid of them and I feel sorry for them. *(She stops looking.)* They make me feel threatened, they put me in a bad mood. *(Pause.)* He doesn't like them either.

EMILIO: Who?

MIGUEL: The boss. Yesterday he sent me to tell them to keep moving…

MARTA: Yesterday? So how long have they been there?

EMILO: Hey, didn't you say your wife was ill? Didn't you say she was in bed?

MIGUEL: Yeah, the missus is not well.

EMILIO: So how come she noticed them?

MIGUEL: How? Good question…there aren't even any windows in her room… *(Short silence.)*

MARTA: She must have felt their presence.

MIGUEL: *(Without conviction.)* Yeah, that must've been it. Maybe they'll get fed up with wandering around before it gets dark, so they'll stop frightening her.

EMILIO: *(Standing up.)* So there's no salvation for anyone.

MIGUEL: *(Almost violent.)* Why do you say that?

EMILIO: Damned by the damned.

MARTA: Damned? Who by? By God? God doesn't damn anyone.

EMILIO: No? *(He looks at her.)* Why don't you take a look around you? *(He goes upstage.)*

MARTA: And what makes you think you're so smart? *(To MIGUEL.)* I've got a stack of rags here, why don't you take them and put them through your machine? I'll sell them to you.

MIGUEL: *(He stands.)* I don't buy rubbish, it's the boss who does the buying.

MARTA: Then I'll give them to you. *(Moving towards EMILIO.)* Mind you they're that filthy they could clog up a railway engine, so they should be fine in your machine.

EMILIO: No, no, no. We may be poor but we're clean; inside and out. And just remember that I pulled you out of the canal. *(Changing his mind.)* No, don't listen to me.

MIGUEL: *(Moving towards them.)* Are you always so nice to each other?

MARTA: No, I've only just met this one.

EMILIO: I wouldn't marry that if you paid me: I know from experience that leads to ruin. Well, that's what I wanted to think… But something in her eyes, or in her heart, or wherever the hell is making me go that way again… But it'll never get anywhere…

MARTA: *(Puzzled. To MIGUEL.)* Was that an insult or a compliment?

MIGUEL: I think he was being really horrible to you. I should dump him right now.

MARTA: *(To EMILIO.)* Did you insult me?

EMILIO: *(He smiles.)* No, I swear I didn't. At least I didn't mean to.

MARTA: Why are you laughing? You've changed, I don't know why yet, but you look happier inside… As if you'd just had some good news.

EMILIO: Sure, he brought it… Didn't you hear him?

MIGUEL: It's not my fault, don't have a go at me, mate: I follow orders. But I'm not your enemy, if I was your enemy, I wouldn't be sitting here talking to you.

EMILIO: Who is our enemy? Do you know anyone? I don't. Everyone loves us several hundred times more than their mother and their grandmother put together; everyone spends their lives fighting for us; they're writing books about us, they're talking about us on the radio, on the telly; they're making laws to help us with this, that and even the other. I swear, I've never known anyone who had a job who wasn't dying to help us out twenty-four hours a day: I mean fuck it, if everyone's at it, if they're all doing the same thing, who the hell is our enemy? Tell me.

MIGUEL: I don't know, that's nothing to do with me, all I know is if I don't work I don't eat.

EMILIO: Well it should be something to do with you, mate; because there are only two possibilities; either it's all one huge piss-take, or our enemy is God.

MARTA: Jesus, that's a bit deep.

EMILIO: Of course, if there's no one on earth who's against us, it can only be Him not letting us go to school, throwing us out of jobs, beating us up and throwing us out of our houses, doing all the other stuff.

MARTA: No, I think it's got to be one huge piss-take, because it couldn't be Him; God is the only one we have, he's the only one who listens to us.

EMILIO: No, he's got no trouble listening, it's answering that's his problem.

MIGUEL: Excuse me for saying this, but I think the problem is that you're very ignorant; He doesn't answer in words, He answers in deeds, He arranges things in a way that no one else could think of. I know that for a fact, mate; he helped me with my missus.

MARTA: But weren't you saying she was ill?

MIGUEL: Yeah, and she's going to die. And I didn't know how to deal with that, because I've always loved her more than anything, and when death walked in and started hanging around I thought that when it took her it would be like it had taken the whole world. Sure, because the death of one person brings many other deaths with it; deaths in the morning, in the evening and at night; half the bed empty – that's one; half the table another…and the words you'll never hear again, that's the death that hurts the most. That's what I was thinking and I didn't know what I was going to do…

Then suddenly she changed, she became mean, she turned bitter; she doesn't give me a moment's peace, everything hurts, everything bothers her. 'Miguel, get me some water,' she says to me and when I bring it to her she has a go at me because it's too cold, or too hot or too lukewarm. 'Miguel, tidy my bedclothes, wipe my sweat, go and see if you can get an appointment with the Social Security. Miguel, I'm hungry, Miguel, pass me the chamberpot, don't drop off; pass me this, pass me that, Miguel, Miguel, Miguel,' she's driving me crazy, she doesn't let me rest day or night. Right now she'll be calling me for some nonsense. And now I've got to tell them *(He points.)* to get lost, it's only going to get fucking worse… So… Of course, I haven't stopped loving her… But it'll be so fucking quiet when she's gone!

EMILIO: What's good about that? Instead of pretending to hate her, you could have tried helping her to get better.

MIGUEL: I don't hate her, pal, understand well what I'm saying to you. But there's no denying that it's been a really shit time.

EMILIO: People who are persecuted but have no enemies, madmen, husbands who welcome the death of their wife, people, *(Pointing.)* lost between heaven and earth, hunger, loneliness, fear… You know what I'd say to God if I met him round here? I'd ask him this one simple little question: 'Hey, pal, why not do unto others as you would have them do unto you'? That's what I'd say to him.

MIGUEL: You've got a real chip on your shoulder, you know that? You don't believe in anything.

EMILIO: You're wrong: I think you should believe in something, but the trouble is there's nothing worth believing in.

MIGUEL: There are times when things just go badly, mate; but you just have to get on with it, isn't that right, lady?

MARTA: Sure, when someone's just died you can tell if life has any meaning because when you're alive things can always change. OK, the water's boiling, pour it into the mugs, they're right here.

EMILIO: *(Pouring water into the mugs.)* She knows what she's talking about, she's the president of the world hope committee… Only yesterday she herself took a running jump into the canal, out of sheer joy at the medal they were trying to award her.

MIGUEL: Did you really throw yourself into the canal? Why?

MARTA: The questions you ask. Don't listen to him.

MIGUEL: And you pulled her out?

EMILIO: Sure, because I'm just so brave.

MIGUEL: So if I'd got her out, she could have been mine. Now the other one's about to kick the bucket, it would have worked out really well for me. *(He touches her buttocks with his club.)*

EMILIO: But I pulled her out.

MARTA: Jesus, so now I'm going to be the scarlet woman; you just go and look after your wife.

MIGUEL: As soon as I've finished my tea. *(He touches her again, moving her to one side.)* If I may. *(He sits in the place she was occupying.)* It's been so long since I've had a moment's peace. Now she's got the idea in her head that she wants to die in her own bed. So she heard that work wasn't going too well and she thinks we're going to be thrown out. That really would be crazy, if you couldn't even die in your own bed. Good job the boss has put me to work on the machines as well as being security guard.

MARTA: So you must be getting good money.

MIGUEL: No, it's just the same, but I get to keep my job; you know how things are out there. But the boss isn't bad, as soon as he heard that my wife was ill, he told her she could stop sorting the rags. And if the sales figures are good at the end of the month, he'll actually pay my National Insurance so I don't have to keep trying to convince the hospital my wife is destitute and they'll give her a bed

EMILIO: So, you're going up in the world big time.

MIGUEL: Given how things are, I can't complain. *(Pause. Serious.)* You know something? *(He stands up aggressively.)* I'm never sure if you're making fun of me or not: why don't you just say things straight out?

EMILIO: I didn't say anything. If there's something bothering you don't take it out on me.

MIGUEL: There's nothing bothering me!

MARTA: He's doing this because his wife's ill, don't you get it?

MIGUEL: What do you mean I'm doing this for my wife? I've always worked!

MARTA: Keep your shirt on. I was telling you about how me and Mario were made to work for whatever they wanted to give us and we just had to put up with it. It's called life, what can you do about it? And it's not even your fault, because you're doing it out of love for your wife.

MIGUEL: What's not my fault, for fuck's sake? What the hell are you talking about?

MARTA: OK, OK, don't get worked up, you'll put yourself into an early grave. I knew someone more or less in the same boat as you. He was married with four children. *(Pause.)* They lived in this horrible ruined old house, in San Isidro Street. And they weren't the only ones, were they? There were about fifteen families; so the house, which had two floors, was full of kids, clothes hanging out to dry, drunks and women fighting for space on the balcony to hang out their clothes.

MIGUEL: *(Drily.)* You mean it was a tenement.

MARTA: *(Dignified.)* No, it was a house.

EMILIO: *(Looking.)* It reminds me of the Jews… Looking at those people over there reminds me of the Jews…

MIGUEL: You mean the Gypsies. You think you're so smart and you don't even know any history.

EMILIO: No, I mean the Jews; Gypsies tell your fortune and make copper frying pans. It was the Jews were who had to wander in the wilderness.

MIGUEL: Jews, Gypsies, what difference does it make? All I know is if they come to the house too much I beat the shit out of them.

EMILIO: I like the Jews, they've got the secret of unity in their blood. Do you know what that secret could be?

MARTA: Excuse me, I was talking!

MIGUEL: Sure, you carry on, it wasn't me who interrupted you.

MARTA: *(About EMILIO.)* This one doesn't like the things I talk about, he doesn't want to get to know me.

MIGUEL: *(Aggressively.)* You just carry on, he's not in charge round here.

EMILIO: That's what she thinks, but she's wrong. *(Pause.)* What's your name?

MIGUEL: *(Surprised.)* You don't even know her name?

EMILIO: No, what's your name?

MARTA: Marta.

EMILIO: *(To EMILIO.)* I'm Emilio. What about you?

MIGUEL: No, I'm not Emilio.

MARTA: *(Laughing.)* Good one!

MIGUEL: Well, you've got to have a go, haven't you, just to wind him up.

MARTA: So what is your name?

MIGUEL: Miguel.

EMILIO: Marta, Miguel and Emilio; OK, now we've introduced ourselves. I feel right at home. *(To MIGUEL.)* Well, what she says is that wherever you are, that's your home. What do you reckon?

MIGUEL: Don't get clever with me, matey, don't try and get smart with me.

EMILIO: You don't believe that? You don't think that if someone is born, they have to be somewhere? What else would we do, those of us who don't have the money to pay rent? Kill ourselves?

MIGUEL: *(To MARTA.)* Please go on; I'm listening to you because I don't want to be rude, I should have gone by now.

MARTA: No, it's doesn't matter, it's nothing.

MIGUEL: Just say it; he's not in charge round here, I'm telling you.

MARTA: No, it was only this: one day the wife of that man I was telling you about got ill like yours, and just when she was about to die, he came home loaded down with parcels and happier than a pig in shit; he brought everything, clothes, food; toys for the children, and all brand new, it was total happiness. So much so that his wife started to get better just from the happiness…or maybe it was just having something to eat. 'You're gonna have to learn to put a smile on your face, old woman, all our troubles are at an end for good,' he told her, 'We've had a bit of a Yankee! A bit of a Yankee!'

MIGUEL: What, on the horses?

MARTA: Uh, yeah, I think so; anyway after that everything was hunky-dory, good clothes, good food, sleeping in beds… Like real people… It was a fucking beautiful thing… *(She falls silent.)*

MIGUEL: And then what happened?

MARTA: *(Lost.)* Hm?

MIGUEL: What else, what else happened…? I have to go in a minute.

MARTA: Nothing… The next week, they came for him, he hadn't won anything on the horses, he'd robbed one of the big houses where he used to polish the floor. 'So what,' he said when they took him away, 'I wasn't going to let you die without knowing real happiness: we're people too.'

EMILIO: That must be your dad you're talking about; you were telling me about when they took everything out of your room. Sent to prison for stealing a little happiness. *(He stands and unhurriedly faces MIGUEL, who gets annoyed.)* It's a wonderful world, isn't it? *(He goes upstage.)* I wonder when this all began and why? I mean to begin with we were all equal, so there was no such thing as an underclass or poor people; we were equal and we were all going the same way.

MIGUEL: Which way's that?

EMILIO: I don't know. We're children of fate, we had no control over our own creation; we were created and told 'Here you are, you have to go that way,' but no one told us why we'd been created or why we had to go that particular way we knew nothing about... Except the only certain thing being that we were going to die...

MARTA: Now what are you on about?

MIGUEL: He's a fucking weirdo. *(Examining him.)* The light's on, but no one's home.

EMILIO: The more I think about it, the more I get the picture...; it's not dying that's hard, that's what we were created for; the hard thing is being born; because you're not born when you're born, you're born when you're truly alive... If you want to live, you've got to change the world. *(Pause.)* Anyone who wants to live has got to change the world. Where did that come from? Where did I hear that? It's fucking true, though... *(Lost in thought.)* Yola and I never managed to change the world...

MARTA: Who's Yola?

EMILIO: Yola...? I don't know, she didn't want to be born.

MIGUEL: *(After a short pause.)* You know what? I'm off. I don't like getting involved in marital squabbles.

MARTA: *(Stupidly.)* You're going?

MIGUEL: *(Smiling.)* That's what I just said.

MARTA: No, I just meant in case you want to take a little tea to your wife.

MIGUEL: No, thank you, she's awash with all the tea I'm giving her already. *(He gets out a pack of cigarettes.)* Do you smoke?

MARTA: Sometimes. If you want you can give me one for the road. *(She takes it.)* Thank you.

MIGUEL: *(Looking upwards.)* Yeah, you should go soon. If you don't you're gonna get a lot wetter than if you do. It looks like rain.

EMILIO: If we have to get wet, we have to get wet. It's the will of God.

MIGUEL: I'm going to smoke this cigarette and then I'm off. I can't smoke over there. *(To MARTA.)* I don't know how, but the boss always knows everything that's going on. Anyway, I guess he's right, it's dangerous to smoke over there, working with all those rags and stuff. *(Pause.)* Which way are you going?

MARTA: *(To EMILIO.)* Which way are we going?

EMILIO: Can I ask you a question? A short time back, I was going over it in my mind.

MIGUEL: Yeah.

EMILIO: The machine your boss put you to work on… Is it the same machine the weaver who vanished used to work at?

MIGUEL: Why?

EMILIO: You said I could ask.

MIGUEL: Well it couldn't be switched off. If a machine stops, it holds up production and if production is held up there are no profits. And if there's no profits…

EMILIO: You see? I was asking why… *(He points.)* What if they were dead, pal?

MARTA: What do you mean dead, can't you see they're walking around?

EMILIO: That's all they are doing though. *(To MIGUEL.)* Didn't you say your wife couldn't see them, but she knew they were there and got scared? And didn't you say you'd seen that master-weaver? Maybe he was on his way back to work… Or maybe he was coming to accuse you of something.

MIGUEL: Do you think I'm stupid? When you die, they stick you in the ground.

EMILIO: Where? Where in the ground?

MARTA: Stop scaring him. And stop scaring me too.

EMILIO: Who do you think they are? Dead people? Unemployed? Homeless people? People afraid something's going to happen to them? We could be one of them, so…

MIGUEL: That's enough. What are you are asking these stupid things for? You trying to wind me up or something? All I know is you have to leave here. *(A vague pointing gesture.)* Over there is none of the boss's business or mine: so get moving, we've already told you're not welcome.

EMILIO: It may not be your boss's business, but there's always someone whose business it is: it's the same everywhere.

MARTA: Sure, you can only stop somewhere when it's dark, when all the doors are locked; because during the day, they come up to you and say: 'Hey, you can't stay here.' 'Why not?' you ask. 'Because you can't,' they say, 'go somewhere else.' And somewhere else they say the same to you, so you just have to keep moving; and you get tired, tired as a dog, but they keep on moving you on and moving you on… No one ever fucking chose to be poor, no one ever chose to be alive: we were brought into this world, we have to be somewhere in it.

MIGUEL: Yeah, I agree with you; but don't make trouble for me, all that's none of my business.

MARTA: You're standing here telling us we've got to go.

MIGUEL: But I've got orders, see?

EMILIO: Who from?

MIGUEL: What do you mean, who from? The boss.

EMILIO: What boss?

MIGUEL: Are you taking the piss? *(Aggressively.)* Now you're taking the piss.

MARTA: No, it's just him. He's joking. He's not bad, he's not a bad person... I've got to know him.

EMILIO: I'm asking you who your boss is, because all the time you've been here, you've been telling us how he sends you to say these things.

MIGUEL: And that's the way it should be. You don't think he's going to come out here himself, to talk to you scumbags, do you?

EMILIO: But who is he? Have you ever seen him?

MIGUEL: *(After a short pause.)* No. *(Pause.)* Why do you ask?

EMILIO: Why do I ask? He's got you holed up in the world's arsehole, among all those milling machines endlessly working and working, churning out dust and stink; your wife is dying alone in some corner and suddenly the master-weavers start disappearing... But the machines can't stop, so you have to do two jobs, keeping watch and working the machine...

MIGUEL: Shut up! Just shut up!

EMILIO: Who told you to do that? Who are you looking after all this for, like a dog...? You're gonna die alone, just like your wife.

MIGUEL: He pays my wages...! He pays my wages...! You... you've got to have a boss... I'm the same as everyone else, I'm the same as everyone else...

EMILIO: But who is your boss?

MIGUEL: *(Hounded.)* I don't know, I don't know, leave me alone! Stop hassling...stop hassling me! I know what I'm doing, I have to do what he says; the old woman's ill, she's dying, if he gets annoyed with me and kicks me out, we've got nowhere to go! Leave me alone, leave me alone, for God's sake! *(After a moment's hesitation, he picks up the sacks.)*

MARTA: *(Terrified.)* What are you doing? What are you doing?

MIGUEL: *(Violently puts the sacks behind the stick that was being used to support the washing line.)* You can put your junk over here! *(He grabs the club and goes towards EMILIO.)* That's fucking it! I'm losing patience! Are you going or aren't you?

MARTA: *(She puts herself in his way, more surprised than afraid.)* Hey… Where did you say? *(She points.)* Over there?

MIGUEL: Yeah, over there's none of our business.

MARTA: *(Incredulous.)* Over there? Over there? *(She takes a few steps and stands behind the sacks.)* If we stand here, you can't do anything to us?

MIGUEL: No, that belongs to another boss; our part only goes up to here. *(He indicates the stick.)* I always put sticks to mark the end of our patch, *(To EMILIO.)* but there are plenty of scum who take them out.

MARTA: And how come you didn't tell us that earlier?

MIGUEL: You mean I have to do everything for you?

MARTA: *(Happy.)* Look, Emilio; we only have to move a few steps. *(Smiling.)* Do you mind? *(She goes over to EMILIO.)* Come on, up you get.

EMILIO: So that's the promised land? *(Pause.)* Who does it belong to?

MIGUEL: I don't know, the boss of over here, *(He moves to the other side.)* I've never seen him.

EMILIO: Out of the frying pan into the fire.

MIGUEL: What did you say?

MARTA: Nothing, he didn't say anything. *(Smiling.)* He's one of us.

MIGUEL: OK, then. *(He goes back.)* I'm not one of those who has no respect for other people, I respect other people's property. *(He points.)* You need any help?

EMILIO: No thanks. You see I'm not going to be able to go over there; I'm very tired.

MARTA: Don't do this, it's only a couple of steps.

EMILIO: A couple of steps to where? No, thank you very much. I'm grateful from the bottom of my heart. I promise you, if I could I would sob my little heart out from the emotion of it all. But you see, I've had to go just a couple of steps too often. Too often I've had to say yes when I wanted to say no. Too often I've had to choose to be nothing... No, pal, I'm not moving from here.

MIGUEL: So you won't move...? You wanna carry on playing the big guy with me? *(He brandishes the club.)*

MARTA: No, no! Just let us stay here, your boss will never find out!

MIGUEL: I can't, he knows everything, he's always known everything I do...! Anyway I can see this scumbag has been laughing at me the whole time! I'm not some piece of shit, I haven't sold myself to anyone; I just look after what's mine, what I've earned...! I've worked here for years, I'm not going to lose my job because of you...! I'm a man, scumbag, not some piece of shit. I'm not some piece of shit. *(He whacks him once.)*

MARTA: Get up, Emilio, get up.

MIGUEL: Are you going or aren't you, scumbag...? Are you going or aren't you...? *(He thrashes him until he kills him. The deed accomplished, the result is the statement of the absurd; in the background there is only the distant, pathetic murmuring of homeless inhabitants.)*

MARTA: You bastard...you bastard... You didn't have to do anything, who would have known we were only a couple of steps further this way...? Who would have known...?

MIGUEL: *(Mechanically.)* I had to do my job... I had to do my job...

MARTA: We've gone mad...we've all gone mad...

MIGUEL: I'm not a piece of shit… I'm not a piece of shit…

MARTA: What have they done to us…? What in God's name have they done to us?